DUBLIN

1. The River Liffey, illuminated.

Publishing director : Jean-Paul Manzo

Editor : Amélie Marty

Editor for the English version : Mike Darton

Text : Ingo Latotzki

Photographs : Claudia and Ingo Latotzki

Design : Julien Depaulis

We are very grateful to : Irish Tourist Board

ISBN 1 85995 763 3

© Parkstone Press, New York, U.S.A., 2001

Printed in Hong Kong, 2001

DUBLIN

Claudia and Ingo Latotzki

❀ CONTENTS ❀

2. Colourful buildings at sunset.

✤ CONTENTS ✤

3. O'Connell Bridge.

Ireland is the only place in the world where the Three Great Falsehoods remain ever alive, ever convincing:

> This really is my last beer for today.

> The check is in the mail.

> OK, we'll meet at half past eight.

With typical irony, the Irish use these statements to indicate to others that they are quite fond of the occasional alcoholic beverage, they can tell stories with the best, and they have little need for punctuality.

If you know this, you are well on your way to getting around Dublin problem-free.

Only recently has Dublin grown from a fairly small city of less than a million inhabitants into one of Europe's most beautiful metropolises. The innumerable museums, churches, cathedrals, galleries and theaters prove that Dublin is indeed worthy of the title it held for one year not long ago: "Europe's capital of culture." In this coastal city, history is visible at every turn. Historical buildings rub shoulders with vibrant shopping and pedestrian zones – a result of the rapid economic development of the 1990s.

Come with us on a walk through the Irish capital city. It's a city that is actually best explored and experienced on foot. If you get tired along the way, I'm sure we'll be able to drop in at one of the more than a thousand pubs, all of which reckon to provide cheer for the weary and good company for new friends. Indeed, long chats and earnest discussions on the wonders of God and the world are what Dublin's bars are famed for. And that in spite of – or perhaps because of – the Three Great Falsehoods of Ireland.

4. The Parliament Building at twilight.

5. Mural.

6. Coffee-break at the Powerscourt Centre.

7. The Long Room, Trinity College.

8. In the Old Library.

9. St Stephen's Green.

There is one place in Dublin where, whoever you are, you will feel small. That will be partly because you are standing in an enormously long chamber with a high wooden ceiling. But only partly. The main reason will be the incredible amount of esoteric knowledge all around you in this chamber. For some 200,000 books, documents and manuscripts are stored here on shelves that stretch for 210 feet (64 meters) in length, a number of them more than 3 feet (a meter) high.

Not for nothing is the Library called The Long Room.

We are in Trinity College, Dublin's famous old university, founded on the site of a former Augustinian monastery in 1592 during the reign of Queen Elizabeth I of England. For more than two centuries thereafter the College permitted only Protestant students within its hallowed walls to absorb its teachings. Today there are no barriers of religion in this now world-famous university – something taken for granted by the approximately 10,000 students who have to share the vast area of the campus with the hundreds of tourists who visit every day.

Trinity College is genuinely spectacular. The rich green of the meticulously trimmed lawn first draws the visitor's attention – it stays immaculate because no one is permitted to set foot upon it. Through the archway at the Main Entrance, Parliament Square may just be glimpsed, with, to the right of it, the old library and its Long Room. And to the right of that is the Dining Hall which, dating from 1761, has thus been the scene for more than 240 years of refectorial history.

10. Parliament Square, in Trinity College.

11. Fountain in front of the Parliament Building.

12. Arnaldo Pomodoro, Sphere within a Sphere, 1982: Trinity College.

13. Trinity College.

What a contrast there is between these ancient buildings and the milling throng of young people who tread between them apparently heedless of the history all around them. How many of these young people will settle down in Dublin anyway? Yet the time when Ireland's population tended en masse to think only of emigrating is actually long past, and today the nation's capital exhibits no sign at all of the decade after decade when Irish citizens in their hundreds of thousands left the country for pastures new.

After all, the European Union in the late 20th century donated millions of dollars to modernize and upgrade the city. Traditional ways of life, even among families, have changed accordingly. In many families now, for example, both parents work, and the proportion of women in the total workforce is currently on a par with that in other European countries. Moreover, many of the women have studied at Trinity College – in the footsteps of authors Oscar Wilde and Samuel Becket. All of the students are of course familiar with the Book of Kells. This medieval illuminated manuscript is among the most beautiful in the world, created by monks who fled in fear of Viking marauders from the Scottish island of Iona in AD 806 and came to live at Kells, some 36 miles (58 kilometers) north-west of Dublin. The Book has been kept at Trinity College since the 17th century, and today remains the object of considerable reverence. Stored in a glass cabinet, it comprises the four Gospels in Latin.

Its compilers embellished many of the capital letters in the chapter headings, incorporating colorful ornamentation as well as scenes depicting people and animals. Some of the inks they used had to be specially imported from the Middle East because certain colors were unavailable in Europe at that time. Every day there is a long line of visitors who wait to get a glimpse of this literary treasure. And every day sees the next page turned – with the utmost care. To take photos of it is not allowed.

It is certainly something apart from the ordinary everyday world. Mind you, the history and knowledge that surrounds it in the university grounds is hardly ordinary or everyday either. But most universities exude that sort of atmosphere – the sense of being cut off from the world and its harsh realities.

Once you leave Trinity College and enter Dame Street, you will probably find yourself caught up once more among the young and ambitious members of the Dublin population, complete with their cell-phones and suits.
It is not far from there to Christ Church Cathedral, which was commissioned in 1171 by Richard de Clare, the Anglo-Norman conqueror of Dublin, and Archbishop Laurence O'Toole. It replaced a wooden church originally built by Viking invaders in 1038. The property was ceded to the new Protestant clerical authorities at the Reformation.

Most impressive in the Cathedral is the nave, with its beautiful gothic arches and its immensely high ceiling. Some of the tiling in the chapel dates back to medieval times. The Romanesque porch is considered one of the finest examples of 12th-century Irish stonemasonry.
By 1870, however, the fabric of the Cathedral building was in sad disrepair. The task of restoration was handed to George Street who insisted on going back to the original plans. Only the crypt of the former Norman church was preserved in its entirety – and its comparatively cumbersome crudeness stands in direct contrast to the clean-cut lines of the rest of the church that has been restored. Yet there are still vestiges of the original Romanesque construction of the south transept, and the tiled floor – in which no fewer than 63 different patterns are visible – is particularly impressive.

14. Work of art in Dame Street.

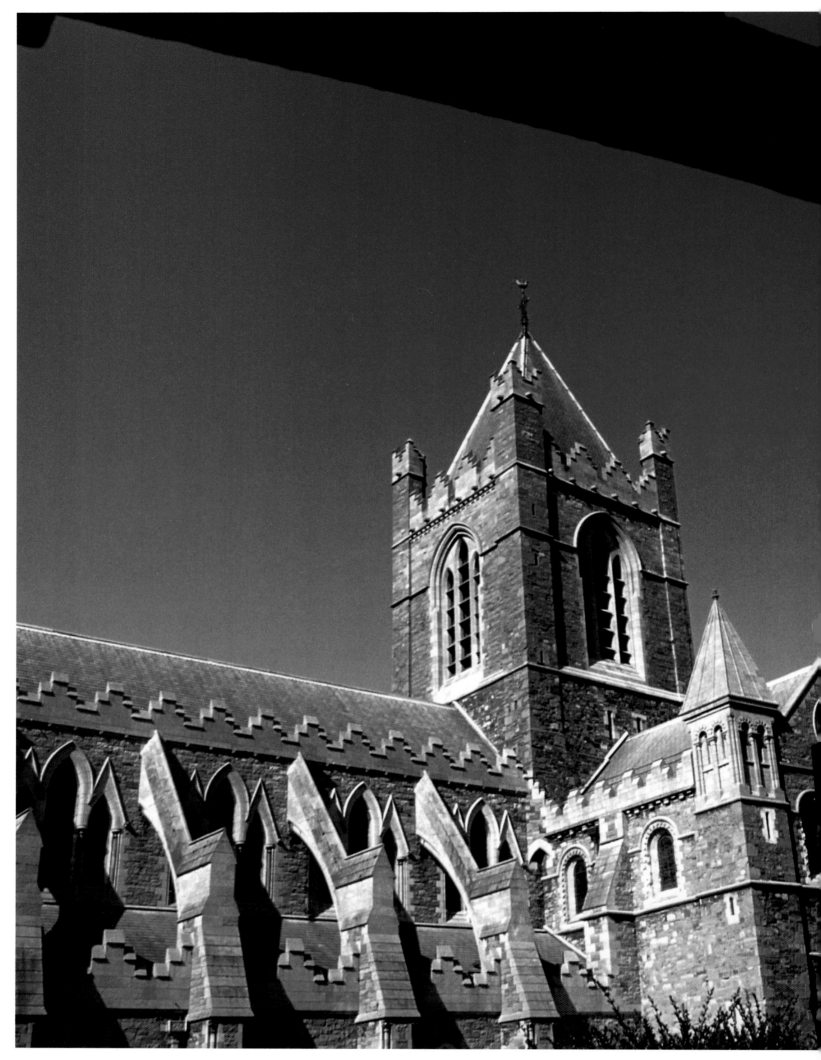

As befits a venerable House of God, traditions continue on – and today, as almost a thousand years ago, choral church services are held every evening. Christ Church Cathedral remains a place of peace and calm, especially in early summer when the flowers come out in full color, and its gardens just invite the visitor to linger.

More prosaically, a mere stone's throw away is the fish-and-chips place held to be the best in the whole of Dublin. But this simply emphasizes the astonishing contrasts in this city: tranquility and furious activity, historicity and modernity, all packed in together. Similarly, some tourist sights may make you feel small and insignificant – but others will make you feel right at home.

15. Christ Church Cathedral.

16. St Stephen's Green.

17. Merrion Square.

18. Evening traffic.

19. Halfpenny Bridge.

Eventide in the merry month of May. It's Tuesday, and the sun shines warmly throughout the day. There is no rain, not even a cloud in the sky, and at Dun Laoghaire beach the sea is certainly warm enough for a swim. But that is exceptional for Dublin. Now, shortly before nine-thirty in the evening, the sun at long last is on its way down. The sky turns to shades of pink and purple that contrast rather well with the warm yellow lights that have just been switched on at and around the Parliament Building.

Darkness in Dublin betokens the time the illuminations are turned on. Many buildings are illuminated at night – so much so that the city never really becomes completely dark. Over the River Liffey, which separates North Dublin from South, the Halfpenny Bridge is lit up so brightly as to be visible from a great distance away. This bridge of cast-iron arches, one of Dublin's great landmarks, is in fact the city's most photographed feature. Built by John Windsor in 1816, it has changed its name several times over the years. Its original name was the Wellington Bridge. Now it is officially the Liffey Bridge – but everybody knows it as either the Metal Bridge or the Halfpenny Bridge (the latter name deriving from the fact that until 1919 there was a toll of one halfpenny to cross it).

The toll ceased a long time ago. No one pays anything, day or night, to cross the bridge now.

Immediately over the bridge is the Temple Bar area – colorful, spectacular, especially as the sun goes down. This is its best time of the day: the blue sky darkens and the first lights pop on in the bars and restaurants. Temple Bar is Dublin's nightclub district, also featuring many fascinating pubs, galleries, and shops, and always thronged with a lively host of people. For that, we must actually thank the artists, the hippies young and old, and other concerned activists, who squatted in the area when it was due for demolition and redevelopment.

" The city is pretty lively. "

ak in Ireland

Discover

26. The Customs House.

But then, Dublin never seems to go to sleep. The streets in the middle of the city are always busy. Groups of people stroll past Trinity College and the Bank of Ireland (the former Parliament Building). "Government buildings are all going to be illuminated," the bartender in one of the bars close to the River Liffey tells us.

One of the edifices whose reflection in the river is particularly clear, thanks to today's fine weather, is the Customs House. This splendid building was erected as the customs and excise office at the end of the 18th century, but within a mere decade or so became redundant when the administration of His Majesty's Customs and Excise was formally moved to London. The building still nonetheless presents a magnificent sight late into the night. Even by day, however, it is not open to the public.

It is not just government buildings that are lit up at night: many churches, hotels, shops and even private residences are illuminated as well. Dublin really wants visitors to see what it is like.

And the city is pretty lively.

Particularly lively are the bars, the pubs, of which there are reputed to be more than a thousand in Dublin (for a resident population of around 1.2 million in the Greater Dublin area). No one has ever really counted them all to see if there are so many – but it hardly matters: there are certainly enough. And very comfortably furnished most of them are too, and full of people even as the clock approaches midnight. At weekends it is often standing-room only, as dusk falls – if you can get inside at all. Most bars are then so packed that it is impossible to tilt your head far enough back to swallow your Guinness. Loud music blares either from speakers or, if you are lucky, from one or other table where a few musical 'Dubs' (as the citizens of Dublin like to call themselves) have come together for a jam session.

Even the bars have to close sometime, though. After all, there is an official closing time – and most pubs observe it . . . in their own fashion. Closing time in summer is officially 11.30, in winter 11.00. No one may enter a pub after that time. But if you are already there, you can stay on – although you are not meant to be able to order (let alone be served with) any more alcoholic drinks.

27. In a pub.

What this means is that the regulars in a bar – and nowadays some of the smarter tourists too – order several drinks each for themselves just before closing time. They can then sit back and enjoy the rest of the night, with their "rations" lined up on the table in front of them. A true Irishman (or woman, for that matter) is certainly not going to let something as mundane as an official closing time come between himself (or herself) and a night's supply of beloved Guinness.

And in turn, this means – at least in mid-summer – that it is often light again by the time the last 'guest' finally leaves the bar. A new day is dawning, the lights illuminating the buildings are switched off, and (with a bit of luck) the sun shines brightly once again.

28. At the bar.

29. A view of the River Liffey in the evening.

30. Patrick Kavanagh, famous Irish author, in one of his favorite spots
    overlooking the weirs of the Grand Canal.

There he is. At first glance, and at a distance, he looks real. He sits on his bench motionless, looking down across the water. He is Patrick Kavanagh, a poet and an immensely likable man. And in bygone days he used often to sit on the bank of the Grand Canal – then in a rather superior area of the city – and, well, just look down across the water. Or that's what they say nowadays about him. Oh, and that he is one of the most significant of modern Irish poets. He actually died in 1967, aged 63. Yet here he sits, his legs crossed, hands on his knees, with his hat and glasses next to him.

Kavanagh is one of the astonishing number of famous and important English-speaking writers from Ireland – although at one stage he was the enfant terrible of his literary scene. Determined not to be regarded by ordinary folk as "upper-class" despite his literary pretensions, he is said to have smeared his boots with cow-dung before entering Dublin so that all would know he was a son of the soil.

In one of his books, he described an act of masturbation. His publisher deleted it from the text. Looking for fame through publication, Kavanagh acquiesced in this censorship. But once the book was on sale in the bookshops, he went into three or four of them, picked up the pristine copies and personally wrote in the missing lines, informing the astounded booksellers and buyers as he did so that the passage had unaccountably been left out of this edition.

A journalist once rather unkindly described him to his face as "only a second-rate poet." Kavanagh responded at once, "But that's true, isn't it, of every poet since Homer?"

The Dublin Writers Museum contains a Kavanagh exhibit, as it contains exhibits representing so many other famous Irish writers. No other nation has been home to so many Nobel laureates for literature. Seamus Heaney was the most recent: others include George Bernard Shaw, W. B. Yeats, and Samuel Beckett. Oscar Wilde and Jonathan Swift were likewise literary giants from Ireland. Swift, "the father of Irish literature" and author of Gulliver's Travels, was born in Dublin in 1667, and is buried in St Patrick's Cathedral.

One of the best-known novels in the world was also written by an Irishman – Ulysses, by James Joyce (to whom there are several monuments in Dublin). It is a difficult book, and a long one (more than a thousand pages in most editions), in which Joyce's hero, Leopold Bloom, actually wanders through Dublin as it was on 16 June 1904. The setting is ordinary, but what Joyce made of it was extraordinary. So much so that that day is still commemorated with great emotion by literary buffs and Joyce fans alike, and known to them accordingly as Bloom's Day.

It is on that day that admirers – one or two clutching tattered first editions of Ulysses – head to the seaside at Dun Laoghaire and the Joyce Tower, a round tower in which the author once spent a few days. On that day too, others walk through Dublin from pub to pub, reciting passages from the work in each, and so follow in the footsteps of the novel's hero. It is a great event!

Many of the great Irish writers have nevertheless been highly critical of their homeland. Jonathan Swift, for example, described the Irish as "a people of traitors and subjects," while novelist George Moore – who preferred to live abroad – penned with irony that

"an Irishman has to flee from Ireland if he wants to remain himself."

But Samuel Beckett was the most scathing:

"France is easier to endure in wartime than Ireland is in peacetime."

Even James Joyce described Ireland as "the sow that gobbles up its young: here there is no life, no naturalness, or sincerity."
It is not surprising that commentators have often referred to the regard of Irish writers for their country as a love–hate relationship.

31. The Grand Canal.

32. James Joyce statue by Marjorie Fitzgibbon, 1990.

33. The Bishop of Dublin.

For some of them, their relationship with the bars of Dublin was undoubtedly one of pure love. Playwright, author and IRA activist Brendan Behan regarded his local pub – Ryan's in Parkgate Street, a watering-place more than 200 years old – as more than a second home. Only his premature death at the age of 41 put an end to his drinking bouts.

34. The James Joyce Tower.

35. A child's First Communion.

36. Statue of James Larkin, activist for Irish independence, in O'Connell Street.

Seamus Heaney, Nobel Prize-winner for literature in 1995, acknowledged the inspiration he gained from a chaser in Davy Byrne's. (A chaser is a tot of spirits downed immediately after a longer drink, such as a finger of whiskey consumed in one gulp after a Guinness). James Joyce preferred Mulligan's – although his Ulysses hero Leopold Bloom went to Davy Byrne's to eat his Gorgonzola sandwich on 16 June 1904. A Gorgonzola sandwich is consumed by all true James Joyce fans on Bloom's Day.

All these stories and more are to be heard on a literary walk around Dublin. Visitors who don't want to go on any of the many literary tours, however, and who would prefer to get away from the city center instead, may amble on down to the Grand Canal and make friends with Patrick Kavanagh on his bench, gazing as ever down across the water.

Appropriate, then, in such a tranquil setting to remember how so many Irish writers have been flamboyant by temperament, fiery in nature, and therefore to reflect that (as the old saying goes) still waters run deep.

An old man leans wearily against the wall of a dark brick building. He is in the shadows on a day that is already dark and gray, even though it is noontide, and in his blue jacket and dark trousers he is hardly visible at all. A few yards nearer us is a wooden dray or cart, also dark in color, to which an ancient and somewhat decrepit nag has been harnessed. What a great photo the scene would make! But even as we think this, we realize that hundreds of other visitors to the Guinness Hop Store probably think the same. Still, camera at the ready, we close in on the horse. Then in the background we discern an iron gate on which is the famous Guinness harp logo. The crowning touch! But just before we can click the shutter, the old man pushes himself out of the shadow toward us. He smiles, baring sparse yellow teeth between gaps. And he poses, right next to the horse, still smiling at the camera. He even points at the logo on the gate to make sure we get it in the photo as well.

Oh well, OK. Click.

37. The Guinness Hop Store. (p. 45)

38. Vat used in brewing Guinness.

39. Apart from water, the main ingredient in Guinness is barley.

That's it. But before we can say thanks and goodbye, the man stretches out his hand, palm upward, to us. There are a few coins on his palm. Suddenly his meaning is all too plain. We give him a punt (an Irish pound). He doesn't look disappointed – just irritated. We add a fifty-pence coin. His face becomes no more cheerful.

In truth, such encounters are pretty rare in Dublin. But the Guinness Hop Store is a famous tourist site. Indeed, there is a sizable parking lot behind the main building, with room enough for several large coaches.

And of course the dray (the flat cart) is itself a historical remnant. Such drays used to be common sights in the city, conveying enormous casks of the beer properly described as 'stout' down to the ships in Dublin harbor. Such casks can still be seen at the Hop Store in St James' Gate, where of course visitors can also sample the pitch-black stout with its beige 'head' (froth). Guinness is made from barley, hops, yeast and water, although it is brewed not here but some distance away. The water comes from streams in the Wicklow Mountains to the south of Dublin – and not from the River Liffey, as many assume.

The Guinness parent brewery in Dublin produces 370,000 gallons (1.4 million liters) of stout every day, of which 40 percent is destined for export. Guinness is on sale in 120 countries, and 22 breweries make it under licence abroad. Most visitors believe Guinness is Ireland's national drink. But that is actually not true: tea is.

Established in 1759 by Arthur Guinness, the company has developed into something of an empire. In addition to stout it brews other types of beer, and has financial interests in Scotch whisky, motor vehicles, meat, pharmaceuticals and publishing. (Until very recently, in the latter regard, it was the proprietor of the world-famous Guinness Book of Records.)

The pitch-black stout has a true home in the Republic's capital, for Dublin is the city of pubs and bars, and every one of them pulls pints of Guinness – the staple diet of many customers – from several taps at once. The locals, the Dubs, have long regarded it as a mystical, almost sacred, brew. And from a trans-Atlantic viewpoint there is no doubt that a pint of Guinness in Dublin has something extra – the Irish pint is larger than the US pint (56 centiliters as opposed to 47).

Another beverage of which the Irish are supremely proud is Irish whiskey – spelled with an 'e', unlike Scotch whisky. Naturally, the Irish claim to have invented the drink before the Scots. Lectures on the subject – with some potentially expensive practical applications – are available (sometimes unstoppable) in Dublin bars.

40. A thirsty horse.

41. Guinness rules! House façade in Dublin.

42. Dublin is the city of bars and pubs: the city contains more than a thousand, so they say. (p. 50)

43. The Old Jameson's Distillery. (p. 51)

The Old Jameson Distillery, located in the Smithfield district north of the River Liffey, is today a museum. Whiskey was distilled here from 1780 to 1971. A video explains the production process. The film is titled Uisce Beatha, which is Irish Gaelic for 'Water of Life'. Because non-Celtic tongues were unable to wrap themselves around the second element beatha (classically pronounced 'baw-ha'), the first element uisce ('water') became the drink's name all over the world.

Equally enlightening is information available at the Guinness Hop Store. Its statistics declare that the Irish on average each drink 25 gallons (94 liters) of stout or other beer every year – less than Germans, Danes or Englishmen. In wine, on the other hand, one Frenchman consumes an annual average equivalent to almost 30 Irishmen together. But tea is what Irish people drink most – 53 gallons (200 liters) per person per year. Even the English don't drink that much.

All the same, the inhabitants of the Emerald Isle spend no less than one-eighth of all their income on alcoholic beverages – mostly on Guinness.

The Guinness brewery is held in great esteem by residents of the city. Brewery workers made redundant by the company's rightsizing have been allowed to remain living in the district of Liberty that was specifically redeveloped by the beer group for its employees. In 1880, the Guinness family donated St Stephen's Green Park – now prime real estate in the city center – to the municipality. The brewery also sponsors some annual events which the poor of the city are encouraged to attend.

It was in the light of this largess that local author Oliver St John Gogarty stated in 1925: "[The] large brewery ... has done more for Dublin than any other of her institutions. What a wonderful connection Guinness creates: you can drink for better living conditions of the poor; you can drink in St Stephen's Green, or you can at least drink in recognition of those who gave the city this park; you even can, if you want to, drink yourself into poverty and turn yourself into the object if no longer the giver of charity."

Leopold Bloom, hero of Joyce's Ulysses, commented quite differently: "Vats of porter, wonderful. Rats get in too. Drink themselves bloated as big as a collie floating. Dead drunk on the porter. Drink till they puke again like Christians. Imagine drinking that. Rats: vats. Well, of course if we knew all the things."

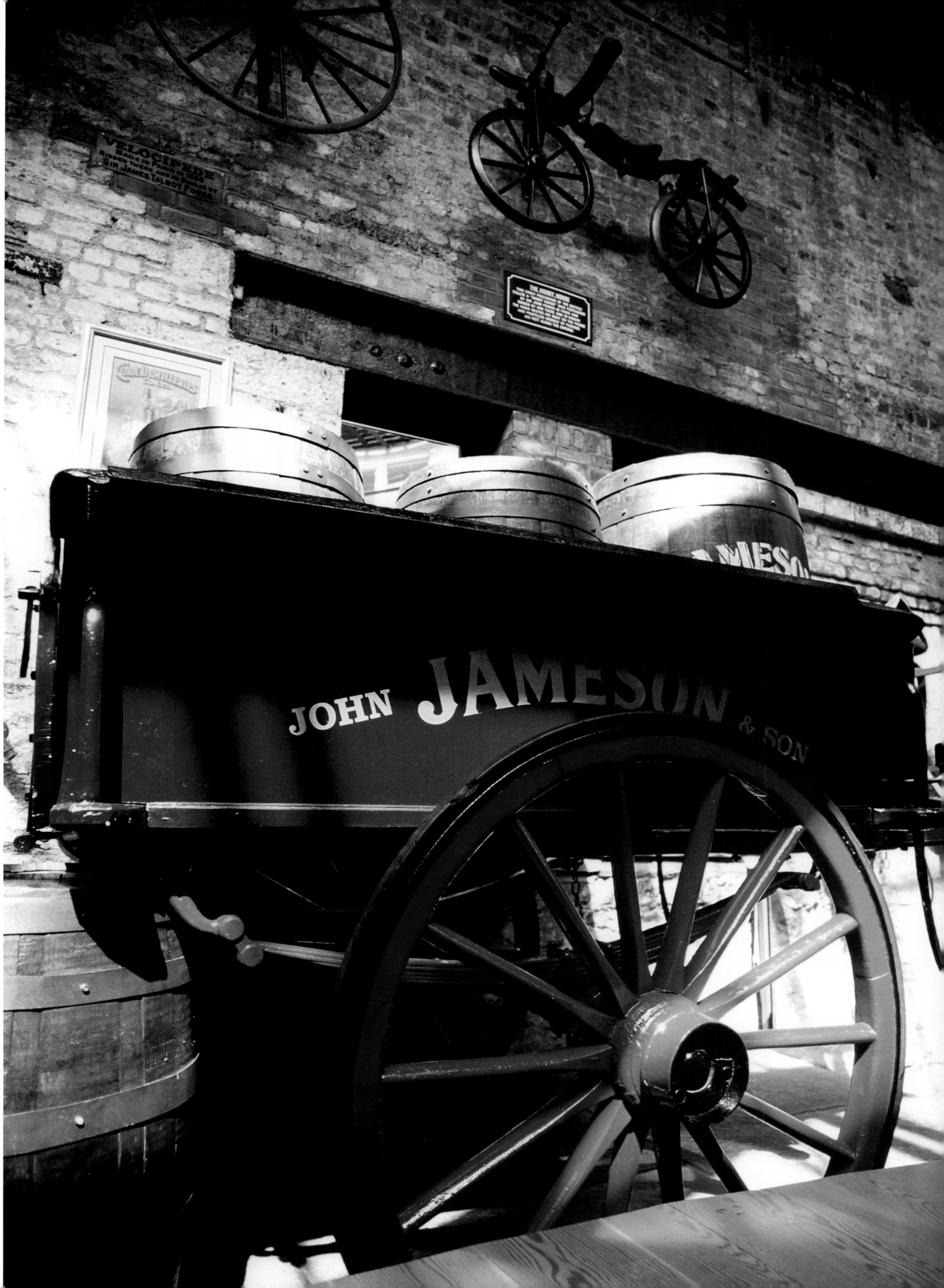

49. Memorial statue on St Stephen's Green to the effects of the Great Famine during the 19th century.

50. Kilmainham Gaol, formerly Dublin's main prison.

What we do know is that the old man who ambushes camera-wielding tourists at the Guinness Hop Store day in and day out would scarcely approve of these lines. If the tourists were to believe James Joyce, the oldtimer with his horse-dray might as well move straight into the Dublin poorhouse.

Stone. Smooth, flat stone. The floor is made up of large stone slabs. The walls are brick covered in beige plasterwork. Connecting them are enormous steel doors. A steep staircase with iron treads leads up two further floors. There again nothing but stone, brick and steel. Thick bolts bar the path to the outside, to freedom. For this is Kilmainham Gaol – Dublin's main prison from 1789 on.

Today, though, it is simply a historic monument, a silent witness to events of the past. Eamon de Valera, who many consider led Ireland to independence, was its last prisoner. Released on 16 July 1924, he was later to be elected President of the Republic.

Dublin displays its history at almost every step and turn. In close-up and full color. The situation in Ireland today – familiar to most of us in the newspaper and TV pictures of sectarian terrorist atrocities generally farther north – is nonetheless also historically represented even now in the city. At the very beginning of O'Connell Street (one of the widest city streets in Europe), with the River Liffey in full view, the statue of Daniel O'Connell stands tall against the sky. With grave dignity it invites tired tourists to rest themselves for a while on its steps.

O'Connell is sometimes given the title "the liberator" because he championed the rights of Roman Catholics in Ireland during the early 19th century. In 1818 he was elected to the House of Commons in London – but was prevented from taking his seat as a member of the Roman Catholic Church. Following enormous popular demonstrations he managed to achieve some measure of Catholic emancipation. In 1841 he was elected Mayor of Dublin.

To step into the busy main street named for him is to step into Irish history. Just a few yards farther down – on the left, if you're coming from the Liffey – is another focus for history-lovers: the General Post Office.

For this post office building (built in 1818 by Francis Johnston, with its neo-classical frontage and stately portico) remains a symbol of the Easter Rising of 1916. It was here that Irish fighters for independence first proclaimed an Irish Republic. The rebels occupied the post office for a whole week before they came under heavy fire from British troops and had to surrender. Fourteen of the leaders of the Rising paid dearly for their pretensions: a short while later at Kilmainham Gaol they were executed by firing squad.

The execution was the start of some bloody times in Dublin. In itself, however, it represented yet another climax to the conflict between British and Irish, and latterly between Protestants and Roman Catholics, that had lasted for centuries already. As early as in 1169 Henry II of England had had considerable interests in Dublin. Those interests grew, until by the 16th century the whole of Ireland was under the sway of the English Crown. Henry VIII then dissolved all the Roman Catholic monasteries and Protestantism became the order of the day. In 1690 the Dutch Protestant King of England William of Orange defeated the exiled Catholic James II at the Battle of the Boyne, north of Dublin – a victory that is commemorated annually to this day in Northern Ireland. London went on to exercise even more power and control.

51-52. Kilmainham Gaol.

53. Statue of Daniel O'Connell by John Folley.

54. Daniel O'Connell.

55-56. The General Post Office.

These events have had their repercussions from that time till now. The first major revolt against British rule was in 1803, when Robert Emmet took up arms intending to besiege Dublin Castle (built in 1205). One of the leaders of the protest movement dating from that time was the aforementioned Daniel O'Connell, whose statue we have already seen in the major thoroughfare named for him, close to the General Post Office.

But even then, Arthur Griffin had founded a newspaper he called Sinn Féin ("We [for] ourselves") several years earlier. The name became that of a movement and later that of a political party which today represents the political wing of the Irish Republican Army, or IRA for short.

It was following the Easter Rising that the movement toward political and national independence really got off the ground. Public sympathy had been strongly aroused for the cause by the executions summarily carried out on the leaders – and by the fact that Britain took it for granted that levies of Irish troops were available for inclusion in the British army. The party won two-thirds of all the Irish seats in the House of Commons in London at the next elections. And Michael Collins – a co-founder of the IRA, and in the eyes of some modern historians a "proto-terrorist" – became Finance Minister.

It was Collins who, on the morning of 21 November 1920, ordered the murder of 14 people identified as British secret agents. Later the same day British soldiers opened fire at Croke Park Stadium during a soccer match between Dublin and Tipperary, killing 12 spectators – an act of apparent vengeance that was thereafter referred to in Irish history as "Bloody Sunday".

Michael Collins is buried at Glasnevin Cemetery, Dublin's largest graveyard. Its vast area is the last resting-place of 1.2 million former inhabitants of the capital. And by historical coincidence, its founder in 1832 was none other than Daniel O'Connell, whom we have met before more than once.

57. Cork Hill, Dublin Castle.

58. The General Post Office, site of the insurrection in 1916.

59. Dublin Castle.

A monument to him stands close to the entrance, visible from some distance. Over his tomb a tower 166 feet (51 meters) high reaches up into the Irish sky.

Other graves feature the typical Celtic crosses (with the cross-joint encircled) in gray, white and weathered stone, some in dilapidated condition. A publicity leaflet there advises visitors to hang on tightly to their valuables in certain zones of the extensive cemetery. But such zones do not include the section where Eamon de Valera, former Prime Minister and President, is buried. Nor do they include the section where many small candles frame the grave of Michael Collins. Playwright Brendan Behan is buried here too, as is Charles Stewart Parnell who made strenuous efforts to further the cause of Irish Home Rule and independence. He has his own monument at the end of O'Connell Street, where a street and a square are also named for him. Many other prominent citizens are interred in Glasnevin Cemetery. Trees shading the paths between the graves include an unusual giant Californian redwood and a cedar of Lebanon – but most of them are the much more familiar maples and oaks.

Nowadays the Cemetery has a security guard, but that has not always been the case. In the 19th century body-snatchers and grave-robbers were not uncommon. Surgeons paid good money for fresh corpses to practice on, as did doctors to obtain specimens for research. Only when it became legal (under strict conditions) for cadavers to be used for research purposes did desecration of the graves finally cease.

Just as death-dealing was the vicious infighting, virtually civil war, that broke out in 1922. The Anglo-Irish Treaty had been signed the previous year and had given the Irish Free State that then came into existence some limited measures of independence. Its members of parliament nonetheless had to swear allegiance to the British Crown.

60. Glasnevin Cemetery, Dublin, where more than 1 million people are buried – among them, Michael Collins.

Six of the nine counties of the province of Ulster seceded from the Irish Free State (to become today's Northern Ireland). At the request of Eamon de Valera, the primary negotiator for the Irish independents in London had been Michael Collins – but it had been strongly against his own inclinations. He had evidently foreseen that radical elements would be unsatisfied with the Treaty and would regard him as a traitor to the cause. Those who supported the Treaty and those who insisted that Ireland should be a united nation took up arms against each other – Irishman against Irishman, without any British participation.

The Four Courts, a courthouse building completed in 1802 on the bank of the Liffey, was occupied by opponents of the Treaty. Free State troops led by Collins bombed the building and besieged O'Connell Street. Collins was gunned down by IRA defectors on 22 August 1922. In May the next year, de Valera denounced the Treaty's opponents, left Sinn Féin, and over the next four years established the Fianna Fáil ("Soldiers of Destiny") party – which won the elections of 1932. The Republic of Ireland was duly founded in 1949.

On the whole, Dublin has been and still is untouched by the tragedy of political events in Northern Ireland. But there have been one or two exceptions. In 1966 the IRA blew up Nelson's Column in Dublin – a column actually higher than the more famous one in London's Trafalgar Square. In 1972, in retaliation for another "Bloody Sunday" in Londonderry in January (where 14 demonstrators were shot down), the British embassy in Merrion Square, Dublin, was set on fire and razed to the ground.

Some traces of these dramatic events remain visible on a walk through Dublin today. Houses on O'Connell Street still sport bullet-holes. At quite a different level of drama, Kilmainham Gaol has served as a setting for several movies, including the award-winning In the Name of the Father (1993).

61. The Daniel O'Connell Tower in Glasnevin Cemetery.

62. Reflection.

63. Statue in O'Connell Street.

Another significant event in Dublin's history is the award of the title Cultural Capital of Europe for the year 1991. That was what inspired the Temple Bar area's current popularity. And since then Dublin has expanded further – although with that has come more crime, more drugs, especially in Dublin's poorer districts north of the River Liffey. South of the river, life raves on. This is the modern cosmopolitan part of the city, where a visitor's casual glance espies little of the bloody events of the past, the tensions between British and Irish, between Irishman and Irishman, and between Protestant and Catholic. The only truly and noticeably sinister element south of the river is the one-time prison, Kilmainham Gaol.

64. Advertisement for the Music Festival, an important event in Dublin.

65. The River Liffey at dusk.

She really did say it. We couldn't believe our ears, but one morning our landlady said, "Last year, summer was on a Tuesday." And she grinned at us. The birds chirp and twitter outside; the leaves on the trees are emerald green; ths sky is bluer than blue – it's a wonderful morning in May.

The springtime sun has been bathing Dublin in mellow yellow light for several days now. And the proprietress of our bed-and-breakfast in the elegant suburb of Ballsbridge goes on to say, just as amazingly, "Well, this is probably our summer for this year." The Irish, it seems, really enjoy only two days in the year: Christmas, and summer.

Maybe that's going too far – it's a cliché with no truth in it. Yet it is true that many parts of north-western Europe are all too familiar in their TV weather forecasts with hearing day after day, month after month, that there is "a Low approaching from Ireland . . ." But that doesn't necessarily mean that it is forever raining on the Emerald Isle.

66. A view of the Liffey.

67. Market scene.

In fact, statistically, Irish clouds let no more rain fall than do German clouds.

It's just the way it is, here on the periphery of Europe. Mind you, Ireland is a land full of myths and legends, sayings and clichés, some carefully preserved and tended over generations. The Irish can hold their liquor/The Irish can't hold their liquor/The Irish drink a lot. The Irish are redheaded. The Irish are basically lazy . . .

Ah, but in this respect even Spain cannot compete with Irish expressions. Many years ago, so they say, a visitor from the Iberian Peninsula asked a Dubliner whether Ireland had a concept of time as elastic as that represented by the Spanish word manana. The Irishman, shocked at such a suggestion, recoiled in horror. "Good gracious me, no!" he exclaimed. "We don't have an expression anything like so urgent here!"

Instead, they have a summer that falls on a Tuesday. It's an idea that doesn't really matter to us – as long as it doesn't turn out to be true. But it looks as if it won't.

And so, on to Merrion Square, where there are many neat and pretty Georgian-style houses dating from the 18th and early 19th centuries. With St Stephen's Green and Phoenix Park, Merrion Square is one of Dublin's "green lungs." During those rare periods when summer apparently lasts for a few days, hundreds of people visit these green open spaces. They lie on the grass, they picnic, they drink, read, and talk. That's taking it easy in Dublin. Even suit-and-tie sits down on the mossy sward of St Stephen's green and rolls up his trouser-legs to dangle bare feet in the water of a fountain.

Traffic continues to bustle past close by – but you don't notice the cars. Their noise, their fumes are absorbed by the luxurious foliage of the large trees planted specifically to separate the street from the park.

68. Market scene.

69. St Stephen's Green.

70. Merrion Square.

71. The Anna Livia Fountain (1988) in O'Connell Street.

72. In a pub.

St Stephen's Green is an area of roughly 57 acres (23 hectares) of parkland laid out at the end of the 19th century. It is a place where people can relax and forget the hurly-burly of modern Dublin. The well-maintained park was a gift to the city from the brewer Arthur Guinness. In a way he is partly responsible for the oft-occurring suggestion that Irish people all drink immense quantities all the time. Guinness in 1759 founded the brewery that still carries his name and that still produces his special kind of stout (or porter) with its bitter taste and its creamy beige head. Skilled bartenders in the multitudinous Dublin pubs are adept, when pulling a pint, at finishing off by creating a cloverleaf shape in the foam on top.

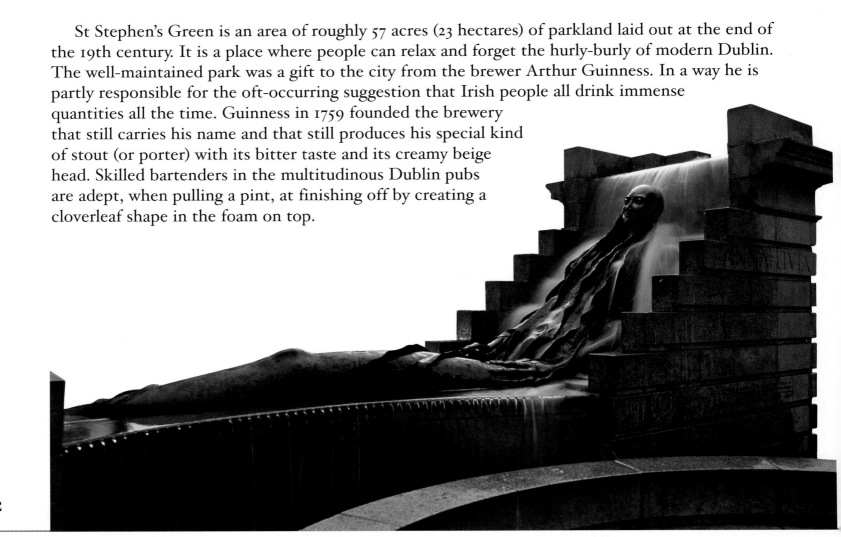

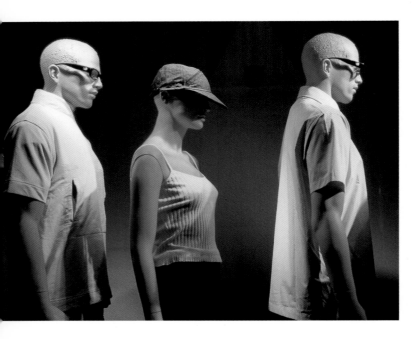

But it's way too early for us to be thinking of downing a pint. One of Dublin's major shopping streets – Grafton Street – starts just opposite St Stephen's Green. Its window displays show how much Dublin has changed over the past few years. As recently as the beginning of the 1990s Dublin was a small city, with fewer than a million inhabitants. Those days are long gone. Boutiques and fashionable shops now stock all the latest goods. Designer-jackets are draped over crimson mannequins lit by neon lights. Mobile phones are ubiquitous – many children wouldn't be seen without one. The phones' tinny chimes and electronic tones are to be heard all over the place, from restaurants to restrooms. Global corporations in high-tech industries have established offices and branches in the city. They furnish additional proof that Dublin is experiencing something of an economic boomtime – thanks, certainly, in part to the billions of dollars donated by the European Union and the confidence of unknown numbers of private investors. Dublin cannot be described as a sleepy little city any longer. Its rate of unemployment, measuring some 20 percent at the end of the 1980s, dropped to just 4 percent by the beginning of the new millennium. And the prospects for work are good. According to pundits, the number of vacant jobs is set to rise. Already, many stores have put up notices in their windows advertising for staff on an immediate and urgent basis.

73-74. Colorful shop windows in modern Dublin.

75-76. Newspaper kiosk: the Irish Times is one of the most
popular daily papers.

Of course, all this prosperity has its downside as well. The number of homeless people is increasing steadily. The crime rate is also rising fast – as is the cost of housing in Dublin, sometimes to outrageous levels. Between 1990 and 2000 the prices of houses rocketed up by 300 to 500 percent, depending on the desirability of the location. The real estate section of the Irish Times, one of the leading daily newspapers, is often thicker than the rest of the paper put together. A one-room apartment near the city center currently costs around US$142,000. Small suburban residences start at $118,350. Thousands of Dublin families have put their names down on lists hoping to be allocated subsidized and low-cost housing by the municipal authorities.

Many of these probably take little interest in the cultural elements of their city. Yet Dublin is well provided with museums and galleries, with magnificent and historic buildings, and with churches, theaters, and concert-halls. In that respect, Dublin is a match for any other European city. What other conurbation has produced four Nobel Prize-winners for literature? James Joyce with his epic Ulysses created a literary monument to his city in a way no other city has been commemorated. Joyce himself is immortalized with one monument erected by the city in St Stephen's Green and another in the atmospheric O'Connell Street.

77.   Statue in O'Connell Street.

78.   Dublin harbor, Howth.

79 - 82.   Howth.

All the same, Dublin has very definitely not become a rambling urban sprawl of housing developments and industrial estates. Almost everything worth seeing in the city can be visited on foot within around 15 minutes of walking. There's virtually no distance at all between Trinity College and Christ Church Cathedral. Ditto between the Halfpenny Bridge and the Shelbourne Hotel and the Parliament Building. Such short distances make it easy for visitors to explore the city.

And if you can't find something straight away? Well, it doesn't matter all that much, does it? You'll see something else, meet other people, instead.

Irish people are open, warm, and very helpful. In 1993, during our first stay in Ireland, driving through the city in heavy rush-hour traffic we discovered we did not know the way to Howth, and stopped to look at our city map. Another driver pulled up alongside, spotted the map, and asked whether he could help us in any way. He could, and did. It was lucky for us – but not an exception for a Dubliner. Although today's Dublin appears much busier and life seems to pass at a more rapid pace, the city is certainly not hectic . . . even if people seem to be out on the streets day and night. They are mostly young people, which is actually not surprising, for Dublin is the youngest city in Europe – half of its inhabitants are 30 years of age or younger. These are people who are glad the Temple Bar area exists.

The Temple Bar district close to the Liffey was earmarked for redevelopment a few years back. Plans centered on a large bus depot. Instead, the area now vibrates and pulsates with life as one pub rubs shoulders with another, their façades mostly bright and inviting (as is usual in Dublin). Restaurants squeeze in between the pubs. The Guinness flows. There is live music, comfy overstuffed chairs under massive wooden tables, and all kinds of decorations on the walls. Noise, smoke, and great and cheerful friendliness. It's a wonderful place for young people.

But maybe that's a bit against too. Still, it's a more upbeat idea than the judgment pronounced by our landlady that last year's summer fell on a Tuesday. Especially in light of the fact that it hasn't rained yet.

The souvenir shop in Grafton Street has a poster hanging in its window. It depicts doors – doors from top to bottom and from left to right: red doors, yellow, green, blue, black, and white. Some have artfully crafted ornamentation in brass, thick handles, or gold mail slots. These doors are famous the world over, depicted in every illustrated guidebook to Dublin. Most of them are doors to the magnificent houses dating back to the Georgian Age (1714–1830) in Merrion Square.

The rectangular square is considered a masterpiece of Georgian city architecture. The area was developed in the middle of the 18th century, in large part by John Ensor. It was one of the most select addresses in town at that time.

The 18th century was an era in which Dublin developed into one of the most elegant European capitals – comparable with Paris under Napoleon III. In 1757 a law was issued to demolish old buildings and thus make way for new and wider thoroughfares and for a more uniform street system with squares. This was the high Georgian Age, so called for the four King Georges who sat consecutively on the British throne. Elegance, harmony, regularity, and symmetry were the architectural ideals of the time. Many of the buildings lend historical ambience to the otherwise increasingly modern appearance of the Irish capital. They are well worth a second look.

87-93. A door with a knocker is standard in Dublin.

For example, there is the Bank of Ireland. Surprisingly, the law that enabled the Georgian reconstruction was enacted in this building. Let's start our excursion through Dublin's architecture right here. Many people today claim that the city on the east coast is one of the most beautiful in Europe – and they say so primarily because of the impressive and magnificent architecture of its historic buildings. Until 1801 the Bank of Ireland was home to the Irish parliament.

The neo-classical building with its magnificent colonnade and three entrances was Europe's first bespoke parliament building. Its central block, designed by the Irish architect Edward Lovett Pearce, was finished in 1739 after his death. Above the pediment in the middle are three statues that represent Hibernia (the Roman name for Ireland), Loyalty, and Trade. The three figures above the east front, added in 1785 by the British architect James Gandon, are representations of Wisdom, Justice, and Liberty. Gandon designed quite a number of buildings in Dublin.

A fire destroyed the octagonal chamber of the House of Commons (the Lower House) in 1782. The chamber of the House of Lords (the Upper House) remains. Tour guides point out the coffered ceiling and oak paneling, as well as the tapestries illustrating the Battle of the Boyne and the siege of Londonderry. The glass-crystal chandelier made in 1788 of 1,233 individual pieces is a masterpiece.

Diagonally across from the Bank of Ireland is Trinity College, of which the major buildings still there today were designed by the architects Keane and Sanderson between 1755 and 1759. The university was first established as early as in 1592 but few traces remain from that time. Statues designed by John Foley stand to left and right in front of the arched gate into the campus. These represent the playwright Oliver Goldsmith and the politician Edmund Burke, both celebrated graduates of Trinity College. In the background stands the magnificent campanile, a bell-tower 100 feet (30 meters) high, built in 1853 by the architect of Queen's University in Belfast, Sir Charles Lanyon.

The museum building (1857) at the far end of the grounds on the right, impresses with its Venetian façade. The two-domed roof encloses a wonderfully colorful hall. In front is the Library Square with its red brick building. The house was built in 1700 and is the oldest section of the university still standing. Altogether, Trinity College is the most significant collection of buildings of the 18th to 20th centuries in Ireland.

94. The Bank of Ireland.

95. Forward march! Off to the Shelbourne Hotel.

Dublin Castle is among the famous buildings that were partly renovated or were reconstructed during the Georgian Age. Anglo-Normans built the original keep during the 13th century, but all the buildings of that era have long since vanished, apart from the reconstructed Archives Tower. Sir William Robinson, one of the governors, designed the current layout of the upper and lower castle yards after a fire in 1684. The first floor on the south side of the complex houses some magnificently decorated rooms, notably St Patrick's Hall (1778). These rooms, decorated with Killybeg carpets and Waterford chandeliers, were once the state apartments of the British Viceroys of Ireland.

The church of the Most Holy Trinity, to one side of the campus, was completed in 1814 by Francis Johnston. The Dublin stonemason Edward Smyth carved the 100 heads on the neo-Gothic façade.

The City Hall also dates back to the Georgian Age. Designed by Thomas Cooley, it was actually built as the Royal Mint between 1769 and 1779.

96. Trinity College.

97. Statue of Edmund Burke (1898) by John Foley, Trinity College.

98. Trinity College.

99. Relaxing, in Merrion Street.

Behind its balustrade and colonnaded façade, the rotunda at the entrance has a cupola supported by six pairs of columns. A floor mosaic depicts Dublin's coat of arms and motto ("The willingness of the citizens is the fortune of the city").

The Government building, also dating back to the Georgian Age, is not far from Merrion Square (which, with its pretty town houses and colorfully lacquered doors, is the classic example of its time). Finally opened in 1911, the complex within which the Government building stands represents the last large construction project of the British authorities in Ireland. Its Portland stone façade, blackened by the city's traffic, has recently been renovated, returning it to its former pristine glory. The building has a splendid cupola and four majestic columns at the entrance. Inside are the Cabinet offices, decorated with modern works of Irish artists. A large stained-glass window over the wide staircase features symbolic representations of the four ancient provinces of the Emerald Isle. It was designed by Dubliner Evie Hone for the 1939 World's Fair in New York.

The Customs House, designed by James Gandon, features columns similar to those in the Government building. It was built at the end of the 18th century, and restored between 1926 and 1991. Two pavilions displaying the Irish coat of arms outline the main frontage, with a Doric colonnade in the center. Edward Smyth created the 14 keystones of the arches and entrances representing Ireland's largest rivers and the Atlantic Ocean. The statue on the central copper cupola symbolizes Trade.

James Gandon went on to design another majestic building in Dublin – the Four Courts on the bank of the Liffey was finished in 1802. It was destroyed during civil unrest 120 years later, but the main building was rebuilt in 1932 following Gandon's original plans. Moses, Justice, and Charity are the figures that surmount the Corinthian colonnade consisting of six columns. The four lawcourts actually occupy the two lateral wings of the building. The public has access to the waiting room under the large cupola.

100. Dublin Castle.

101. The way in to Dublin Castle. In the background is the Archives (or Records) Tower, 1258.

102. Springtime in Dublin – a pedestrian precinct.

From here it is just a short distance to another impressive building completed in the 19th century. The best view of St Anne's church is from Grafton Street, and is well worth anybody's time, especially in summer when the street cafés in front of the church are quite busy. The magnificent Romanesque façade is by the two architects Deane and Woodward, and the church was built in 1868.

St Teresa's church is yet another that offers glorious architecture. Its foundation stone was laid in 1793. Approximately 200 years later, Phyllis Burke completed seven stained-glass windows that deserve much more than just a second glance. The exquisite sculpture of Christ below the altar is the work of the artist John Hogan.

Dublin is a city of culture. Historic buildings are to be found in almost every street in the city center. Many of them – as we have said before – date back to the 18th century.

Not far from St Teresa's church is the Mansion House, an attractive building in Queen Anne style. It was built for the aristocrat Joshua Dawson in 1710. The city purchased the house five years later to be used as the Mayor's official residence. Its gray stucco façade dates from Victorian times.

103-104. The National Library.

105. The National Gallery of Ireland.

106. The exterior of the National Library.

107-108. St Patrick's Cathedral.

109.   The Irish Museum of Modern Art.

110.   The Casino Marino and its neo-classical structure.

Built in 1880 by Thomas Deane and equally impressive is the Irish National Museum. Marble columns and a mosaic zodiac decorate the vaulted circular hall. The rotunda with its cupola, in imitation of a much older museum in Berlin, Germany, constitutes a truly magnificent entrance hall.

Deane designed more than just St Anne's church and the National Museum, however. He was responsible also for the National Library which, with its intricate roof cupola, was constructed in 1890. It is here that important first editions of Irish authors such as Swift, Goldsmith, Yeats, and Joyce are housed.

Speaking of Swift (1667–1745), the author of Gulliver's Travels lived into the Georgian Age and was dean at St Patrick's Cathedral, Ireland's largest church. Most of the current building was completed between 1257 and 1270. Minot's Tower, some 150 feet (45 meters) high, looms skyward at the western end of the nearly 300-feet-long (90-meters-long) structure.

The inside contains many commemorative busts, plaques, and tombs. In the old door at the west end of the nave, the strange-looking hole is the result of a feud between Lord Kildare and Lord Ormonde, the latter of whom sought sanctuary here in 1492. The truce agreed a short time later was the occasion for Lord Kildare to cut a hole in the door to shake hands with his former enemy.

One of the most beautiful Georgian buildings in Dublin is without doubt the Casino Marino. The former palatial mansion with its gardens is located to the north of Dublin, out in the direction of Howth. It stands on an elevated terrace of which the corner points are marked by four stone lions. Scottish architect Sir William Chambers (1723–1796) – who, with others, also rebuilt Buckingham Palace, London, and created Dublin's City Hall, today's Museum of Modern Art – drew up the original plans for the house. But the property fell into disrepair over time, and it was not until 1970 that restoration began. The place has been open to tourists since 1984. The whole of the building is embellished with gorgeous Georgian décor.

Innumerable doors can be opened in Dublin. Some doors lead into and out of historically or artistically important scenes. Other doors are just doors – red ones, yellow, green, blue, black, and white. Merrion Square and Grafton Street have plenty of these. But the latter presents these doors only on a poster in a souvenir shop.

8000 B.C.:	First settlement in the geographic area that is Dublin today.
500 – 300 B.C.:	Celts bring the Gaelic language and culture to Ireland.
839:	Vikings from Norway come to "Dubhlinn."
1014:	The Vikings are defeated in the Battle of Clontarf near Dublin.
1169/1171:	The Lordship of Ireland is created. Previously, the British King Henry I let Normans, Flemish, and Welshmen conquer portions of the country. Dublin becomes capital of the British colony in 1171.
1534 – 1541:	Henry VIII decides to be crowned "King of Ireland."
1560:	Elizabeth I declares Ireland a Protestant country (Anglican).
1640:	Most Protestants live in Dublin, most Catholics in the country.
1690:	William of Orange's army defeats the troops of the Catholic King James II in the famous Battle of the Boyne. The Protestant Orangemen of Northern Ireland still celebrate this victory today.
From 1700:	Dublin's "Golden Century." Thanks to the Protestant Anglo-Irish numerous new buildings in the Georgian style are built. Four Courts, today's Collins Barracks, Powerscourt House, Custom House, today's City Hall, Parliament, Trinity's western façade, and the Mansion House.
1797 – 1798:	The revolt of the United Irishmen is betrayed in Dublin. Leader Wolf Tone commits suicide.
1801:	Unification Law: Ireland is now officially a part of Great Britain. The descent of Dublin from Europe's sixths largest city and the second largest city of Great Britain to a provincial small town begins.
1803:	The uprising against the British and the capture of Dublin Castle are unsuccessful. Leader Robert Emmet is executed.
1823/1829:	Daniel O'Connell organizes a mass movement, the Catholic Association. O'Connell ("The Liberator") was the first Catholic elected to the British House of Commons. The anti-Catholic penal laws are lifted in 1829.
1845 – 1848:	"The Great Famine" strikes Ireland; a rural exodus to Dublin begins; the immigration wave starts.
1879 – 1890:	The Protestant Charles Stewart Parnell fights for Ireland's independence and Home Rule.
1913:	Europe's worst slums are in Dublin. Sometimes five families share one house.

1916: Patrick Pearse declares the Republic of Ireland during the Easter rebellion. The rebels have to surrender after six days. Of the rebels, 16 are executed by order of the British crown. After the executions, the public sympathizes greatly with the previously isolated rebel movement. The executed become martyrs.

1918: The nationalistic Sinn Féin party (founded in 1905) wins the elections.

1919 – 1921: War of independence. On 21 January 1919, the Irish Parliament (Dáil Éireann) declares its independence; guerilla fight of the Irish Republican Army (IRA); 6 December 1921: British-Irish treaty – the Irish Free State is founded; the island is partitioned (mostly Protestants live in the northern part).

1922 – 1923: The Republicans split, a civil war ensues. The anti-treaty forces want independence for the entire island. Four Courts is destroyed; a truce is declared in 1923.

1939 – 1945: Ireland remains neutral during WWII. The German air force mistakenly bombs Dublin in 1941 resulting in 28 dead.

1949: Ireland is declared a republic on Easter Monday.

1969: The civil war ("The Troubles") starts in Northern Ireland. Until 1994, 3346 people are killed.

1972: "Bloody Sunday" in Derry. The British army kills 14 unarmed Catholic demonstrators. The nation mourns. Dubliners burn down the British embassy at Merrion Square.

1973: Ireland joins the European Community.

1974: A bomb attack in Dublin City results in 25 dead. Protestant terrorists probably committed the attack.

1976: The IRA murders Great Britain's ambassador to Ireland in Dublin.

1988: Dublin celebrates her millennial.

1991: For one year, Dublin is Europe's cultural capital.

1998: Dublin with its districts has more than one million inhabitants. The peace agreement is approved by 94.7% of all Irish ("Good Friday Agreement"); the "Tour de France" starts in Dublin; on 15 August, in Omagh, Northern Ireland, 29 people are killed and 220 seriously injured. This is by far the gravest attack of the civil war – carried out by a splinter group, the "real IRA."

MAPS

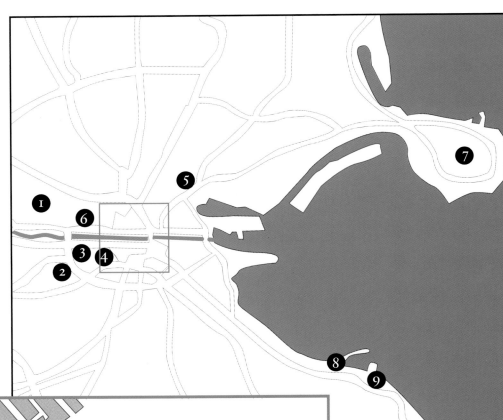

- .1   Phoenix Park
- .2   Kilmainham Gaol
- .3   Irish Museum of Art
- .4   Guinness Hop Store
- .5   Marino Casino
- .6   Collins Barracks
- .7   Howth
- .8   Dun Laoghaire
- .9   James Joyce Tower

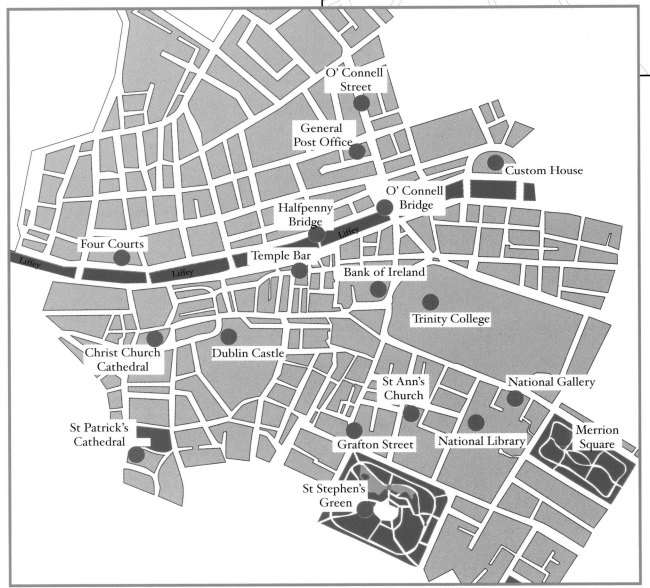